JUGGLING

JUGGLING

All you need to know to develop
amazing juggling skills

STUART ASHMAN

p

About the Author

Stuart Ashman was inspired to juggle in the late 1970s after watching street entertainers in San Francisco. He has subsequently performed in the comedy duo 'The Norfolk Mountain Rescue A Team' and as a solo act all over the world. The organizer of the second British Juggling Convention and publisher of *The Catch* – Britain's juggling, new circus and street theatre magazine – he still travels the globe to take his act to the public from the tiny backwater of the Chew Valley, near Bath.

Editorial consultant: Steve Henwood

This is a Parragon Book
This edition published in 2003

Parragon
Queen Street House
4 Queen Street
Bath BA1 1HE, UK

Designed, packaged and produced by
Stonecastle Graphics Ltd

ISBN 1-40540-407-8

Photography by Pinpoint
Edited by Philip de Ste. Croix
Models: Lisa Ashman, Stuart Ashman, Richard Dwyer

Manufactured in China

Contents

INTRODUCTION

JUGGLING IS no five-minute fad soon forgotten. Juggling is pictured in Ancient Egyptian friezes dating from 2000 BCE; it was among the entertainments at the great medieval fairs and part of the performances of magicians and mountebanks long before that. More recently, jugglers have held down top billing in variety theatres and music halls; many went on to be comic stars of the silver screen; now they have reappeared in the street circus, cabarets and spectacles of the 21st century.

Nowadays you might see jugglers anywhere – a beach, a park or a street corner. Juggling is no longer a closely-guarded secret passed down in circus families or from teacher to apprentice. That's just not the way we do things any more; today it's easy to learn from other jugglers and you are encouraged to do so. This book is part of that process.

Juggling is also, I have to point out, extremely good for your co-ordination and left brain/right brain balance. But better still, it's fun – fun you can have on your own and fun you can share with others. People can be as amazed by your skills as were the audiences in Ancient Egypt and the bazaars of Baghdad. With other jugglers you can swap tricks and work out even more complex ways to juggle.

There's more not in this book than there is in it, but I'm starting to juggle with words and you've just been given three balls to do that with. So let's get going!

THE BASICS

Getting Started

WELCOME TO your juggling book. It's not a book that juggles; it's a book that will help *you* to juggle. It's not really a book to juggle with, but by the end you'll be able to do even that...if it takes your fancy.

Juggling is easy to learn. I've known people to pick it up in half an hour – but most take a little longer, so don't worry if you are not as quick as that. Practice is very important; you've got to teach yourself new habits, just as when you learn to ride a bike, and repetition is the only effective way to do this. The book is designed to introduce you to a new skill on every double-page spread (with a few exceptions which you'll discover along the way). When you are working through the first part and most of the second, it is important that you can do the sequence described on one page before moving on to the next, because the skills build on one another.

Patience!

The book comes with a set of balls that are ideal to learn with – but you can juggle virtually anything, any kind of ball from ping-pong to cannon! Someone is bound to ask you to demonstrate with tennis balls, but you'd better wait until you have mastered the basics before trying that. Tennis balls are very light and bouncy and tend to hop straight out of your hand before you can catch them.

That is not a good way to start. This is.

The Stance and the Jugglespace

THE WAY we stand or sit when attempting any skilful task will affect our performance. Correct posture, if learned and applied at this stage, will help prevent problems developing in the future.

1   Be comfortable. Your feet should be slightly apart, legs relaxed and bent at the knees.
2   Your hands should be at waist level, palms up and held at the side of your body.
3   Shoulders relaxed.
4   Eyes looking straight ahead at a point just above forehead height.

It might help if I introduce an important imaginary concept at this point.

Imagine that in front of you is a sheet of glass, or an invisible frame like those used for windows or pictures. The bottom corners are your two hands, the top is in a line just above head height (see photograph left). For the basic juggling pattern all the balls must remain within that plane, the sheet of glass or the frame (right). I call it **"the jugglespace"** for short. There is no agreement on the use of that word among jugglers in general, but I like it.

STAGE 1

LEARNING THE CASCADE

One Ball

PLACE ONE ball in your stronger hand (the one you normally use for writing or holding tools) with your palm face up, and throw it to the other hand (right). Yes I know it's easy – but take time to watch the arc that the ball makes as it travels through the imaginary plane of the sheet of glass that I told you about on the previous page.

Important Rule No.1: Juggling is about accurate throwing, not just catching.

Try to make your throw with one ball so accurate – the arc of its flight peaking just above head

height – that you don't have to move your other hand to catch it. All throws and catches at this stage should be made palm up and done at waist height (above).

Now repeat this throw with the other hand. If this is your weaker hand, really concentrate on the accuracy of the arc; your catching hand should not have to move much to catch the ball.

Yeah, I know this stuff seems so dull...but it's the ground work to stop you getting stuck on the problem pages later on. Trust me and give it some time.

Two Balls

TAKE A ball in each hand, palms facing up, feeling relaxed, deep breaths – now, as before, throw a ball from one hand to the other. Just as it peaks in that arc you have learned (below), throw the second ball to the other hand (below right). *Wait* before you try this.

Important Rule No.2: The second ball should be thrown up and over to the other hand.

Some of you – and you know who you are – will try to pass the second ball directly to the other

hand without throwing it upwards. At this stage always throw *up* whichever hand you are using.

1. Keep the arcs consistent. Different heights will make one hand rush to catch the ball.
2. Stop after the two throws. Keeping the motion going is a hard trick to be learned later.
3. Count out loud as the throws reach the peak of the arcs:

"One...Two..." It sounds stupid but somehow the brain tells the hands when it is the right time to throw!

Stay practising this stage until your throws are really good; do not turn the page – work, work, work – trust me!

By the time you can work with two balls properly, you are over half way to juggling and already past the hard stage.

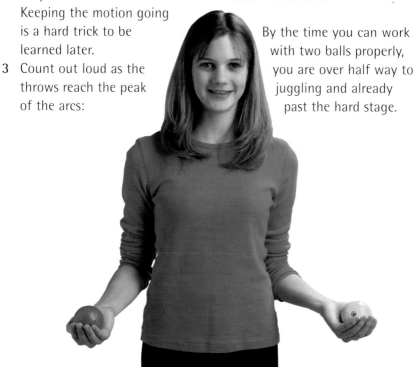

Three Balls

IF YOU *can't* throw two balls with confidence with accurate throws – and no drops – then turn back a page and practise, practise...and practise some more. If you can do it, glad to have you still with us...

Take the third ball, hold it in your strong hand – you now have two balls in that hand (below).

Important rule No.3: Don't panic!

That's all: remember your stance, the jugglespace and the imaginary sheet of glass.

1   The ball furthest away from you in the hand holding the two balls throws first.
2   As the first ball peaks (below), throw the second ball from the other hand – as in the two-ball stuff.

Confused? Just think that each throw is clearing a hand to catch the next ball! Confident? Now try to put an extra throw in. The fourth throw will bring two balls back to the start hand. Why stop now? Keep the pattern going counting your throws to beat your record. You may find you get stuck on one total for a while – we all do – but after 30 throws you can say you are really juggling – because you must have made a few mistakes and corrected them! Time to learn some tricks!

3 When ball number two peaks (top of page), throw the third ball across (above) and catch it in the hand that holds ball one. If you have caught all three – congratulations! You are now juggling!

17

Why Can't I...?

ON THIS spread we'll look at some common juggling problems. Strange but true: not everybody juggles on their first attempt! However, if you have spent at least half an hour trying to get to the third ball, then there are only a few reasons why you are not juggling.

1 I don't have time to throw the third ball.

Sometimes you may find that the second ball is caught in the hand that is still holding the third ball. It has been a lot to take in, so at this stage the brain needs some help to sort things out!

Solution: Counting out loud as the ball peaks on each throw will send a message to your hand and help you to release the ball at the correct time. I don't know why but this does work – but the counting must be done *out loud*.

2 I can't help passing the second ball to my other hand instead of throwing it up (below)!

Even though you have spent time on the two-ball exercise, when

confronted with three balls what I call the old "school yard" throw starts to return.

Solution: Swap the two balls (in the first-throw hand) over to your other hand. You are probably starting with your strong hand, but the weaker hand is usually more open and amenable to learning a new skill!

3 I only drop some throws, not all of them.

You can be tempted to try to catch a throw too early, either by snatching it (catching with the palm down) or trying to take the ball too high (below left and right).

Solution: Wait until the ball is about waist height and catch it palm up.

Why Can't I...?

MORE ANSWERS from the juggling doctor's surgery.

4 I have to move across the room to maintain any sort of juggle (below)!

It can be good exercise but "sprint juggling" as it is called is very frustrating for the beginner.

Solution: Remember the analogy of the sheet of glass (see pages

10 –11). Throwing a ball either forward or behind the correct plane will result in the next throw being even worse. As throws tend to be away from the body, your only option is to reach forwards, and it's a downward spiral from there. Go back to practising with two balls and really concentrate on accurate throws. Standing in front of a wall can cure sprint juggling; it hurts!

5. The balls collide in the air and I'm left with empty hands.

The heart starts to pump and the hands sweat when you have three balls to juggle for the first time – throwing too fast can be the brain's way of trying to cope with the problem.

Solution: As in problem 1, take a deep breath and count out loud as the balls peak to help you establish a comfortable, unhurried juggling rhythm.

6 I simply can't grasp the three-ball throwing sequence in my head!

Solution: Throw all the balls in the correct order (right) but don't bother to catch them (below). The correct juggling pattern will leave two balls together on the floor on your left (if you started with your right hand) and one on the floor on the right (if you started with your left) (below right).

Stage 2

THE WORLD OF THE THREE BALLS

Now We're Started...

WHAT YOU have just learned is called "the cascade" in technical juggler talk. It is the basis of everything that follows.

From now on, although some of the skills in the later pages build upon routines I explain first, there is nothing to stop you trying out two or three different things at once. In fact it's a lot more fun that way. Try and be ahead of yourself, especially when practising a skill that you've nearly "got": vary your practice by putting other moves in, and soon you'll find you are building up sequences of tricks that naturally go together.

Always keep your juggling balls somewhere that you can find them when the fancy takes you – four minutes of spontaneous fun is often better than half an hour of set practice. Juggling with music playing is great too – sequences of moves seem to flow out of the rhythms.

HOT TIP

I have already mentioned counting out loud. Count each ball as it reaches the top of its arc. Even if it sounds daft, it <u>really helps</u> your practice, your rhythm and your concentration.

One last thing. It's always important to master everything you do *with both hands*. That way you can do many more impressive tricks, and make the most out of every new skill. Of course, one hand is likely to be better than the other – in this book we refer to them as the strong and weak hands to avoid confusion. To hop back to our jugglespace for a moment: imagine that it is divided in half vertically down the middle – the central axis of your body (bottom right). Everything that you do on one side of the dividing line should be mirrored on the other.

The High Throw

WHILE JUGGLING three balls it's good practice to try and speed up or slow down the pattern. This is done by altering the height of the throws. Consistently high throws with all three balls will give a slow pattern; low throws will make you juggle faster.

Got that? Perhaps you're ready for your first trick. When trying any new trick it's good to break it down into easy stages.

1   Throw one ball high into the air (right) and practise catching it with either hand.
2   Now hold a ball in the catching hand, releasing it just before you catch the high throw, and throwing it in the normal way to the other hand.
3   Repeat step 2, this time with your other hand.
4   Now try the trick while juggling normally.

HOT TIP

While the high throw is in the air, hold on to the other two balls for a moment - a beat or two is missed in the rhythm of the pattern. The high ball and the delay before the next throw give you time to do more difficult tricks which we'll come to later.

The First Tricks

WHEN YOU send the high throw into the air – whether it's just a short distance higher than your normal pattern in the jugglespace or if it goes as high as you can possibly throw it while still holding some hope of catching it again – you have suddenly given yourself time. Time in which you can do something else; something that nobody expects. This is the beginning of making *tricks* that can surprise and delight yourself or an audience or anyone to whom you're showing off.

So what can you do with that short spare moment? Here are some suggestions. I am sure you can come up with excellent ones of your own.

1 Swap the other two balls over.
2 Bang the two balls together (right), or clap (more difficult).
3 Pirouette – turn right round really fast.
4 Somersault (if you are gymnastic).
5 Sing a little song (whether you are musical or not).
6 Pinch someone's hat, drink or ice cream (if you're cheeky).

Over the Top

NOW FOR your first real trick. Until now all throws have been made underneath the arc of the descending ball, inside the pattern. Now try throwing *outside* the pattern to the other hand: the ball seems to fly over the top of the juggle.

As with most juggling tricks, it is easier to break this down into a sequence using two balls and then extend it to three.

1 With a ball in each hand, throw a normal arc with your weak hand; as the ball peaks, throw an outside throw with the strong hand (pictures right). The second throw will take longer to reach the other hand.

2 Now try it with three balls (page 29). It may seem strange to make the adjustment for the outside arc; more time spent practising at stage 1 will make this seem easier after a while.

Any new trick should be practised with both hands – try to master it with your weak hand as well as with your dominant hand. The same trick performed with both hands produces a *reverse cascade* juggling pattern – and that's very impressive. Or try returning the over the top throw immediately to the original hand with a mirror throw. If you can keep this going, especially with a different coloured ball, it looks great – the ball seems to go backwards and forwards over the other two like a game of tennis.

Under the Leg

ALL THROUGH the book so far I have emphasized the image of the "sheet of glass" (see pages 10-11) and how important it is to juggle consistently in one plane. Now it's time to forget it! After a while you will want to attempt the *under the leg trick* – oh yes you will! Here's how you do it.

with your weak hand should be pitched slightly higher. This gives you valuable extra time to bring your hand down and under your leg (far right) – releasing the ball on the other side with an accurate hop to the other hand – and then back to the front again.

1 Take just one ball in your strong hand, throw it under your nearer leg and over to the other hand. You may find it easier to bend your leg slightly and throw under the knee (right).

2 Now with two balls repeat stage 1, but the second throw is a normal cascade throw to the other hand, which is now back in front. Catch it!

3 Try throwing the normal arc first – then the under the leg throw (top left, page 31).

4 Now juggle with three balls. The throw before the trick

HOT TIP

Remember to count out loud: "one" when the first higher throw peaks, "two" when throwing under the leg, and "three" when you revert to the cascade.

As always, try with the other leg, then practise with both – right/left, right/left. Also attempt throws under the leg on the other side from the trick throw – i.e. under the left leg with the right hand and vice versa.

Behind the Back

THIS TRICK uses virtually the same principles that you have just learned for the *under the leg* throw.

1 Take a ball in your strong hand and pass it in a smooth arc behind your back releasing the ball level with the base of your opposite shoulder blade (i.e. if you are throwing right-handed, the ball should be released behind your left shoulder blade). The ball should continue to travel up and appear to hop over your shoulder (below left) and down into the waiting palm of the other hand.

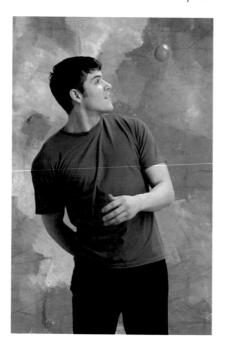

2 With two balls, one in each hand, wait for the trick throw to peak over your shoulder (bottom right, page 32) before releasing the second ball from your weak hand in a normal throw to your dominant hand.

3 As a variation, try throwing the trick throw as the second throw of a sequence.

As always try to master the trick with both hands, then you will be able to do continuous throws with both hands! Juggling without being able to see your hands (below): pretty impressive!

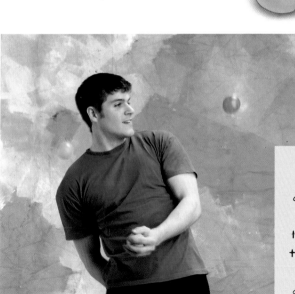

HOT TIP
The shoulder over which you are going to throw the trick throw should be relaxed and dropped slightly for best results.

Two Balls in One Hand

ONE POSSIBLE definition of juggling is *the manipulation of more balls than you are using hands*, so two balls in one hand is definitely juggling.

1   In your stronger hand, hold two balls. As in the *three-ball cascade*, the ball furthest away from you is the first to be thrown in this pattern.

2   Release the ball vertically upwards, throwing it away from the central axis of your body and slightly higher than you would in your normal cascade arc. As it peaks, throw the second ball in the same path as the first (below left).

3   Your hand should then move over to catch the first ball (below), and then the second.

HOT TIP

The imaginary sheet of glass has made a welcome return - the balls will move in a circle in this plane (clockwise using the right hand, anti-clockwise with the left) - you will find out why later! Your hand just makes sideways movements, catching and throwing. Now try the same pattern with your weak hand.

Another way of juggling two balls in one hand is by *throwing in columns*. The balls rise up vertically, falling back down again in the same path or column (right). Time the second throw to happen when the first ball peaks; the throwing hand just makes sideways movements to allow space for the balls to rise and fall.

Tricks with Two in One Hand

WITH YOUR strong hand juggling *two in one* as we have just learned, the other hand can simply throw the third ball vertically in time with one of the other balls, or you can "cheat" the trick by just moving your hand up and down with the ball still in it!

For best results show the third ball with your hand upright and the palm facing away from you towards the audience. Be ambidextrous! If you're solid on doing columns with one hand, then try the same tricks with them too.

One up Two up

1. While juggling three balls, throw one up the middle of the cascade (below), as in the high throw.
2. When the ball peaks, the remaining two balls in either hand should be thrown

simultaneously in vertical column throws (below) which will eventually land back to the same hands.

3 As in the high throw, you can decide which hand will catch the descending centre ball. Sometimes it's effective to alternate the hands that make the catch.

The Yo-Yo

While juggling columns, hold a ball with your other hand over the ball that you are throwing nearest to the central axis of your body (above). Move this hand up and down in time with the ball, thereby giving the impression that the balls are attached by an invisible string. A similar trick features an imaginary magnet.

Stage 3

GETTING FANCY

The Snatch

W E'VE JUST experimented with the way you throw. Now try changing the way you catch.

1 Throw a ball from your weak hand to your strong hand but catch it with your palm down (below and right) – snatch it!

2 Now throw the ball back releasing it with the palm up.

3 Place a ball in each hand, throw the normal two-ball cascade pattern, but snatch the ball with your strong hand, taking it at the peak of the arc.

4   Juggle normally with three balls, and cue the trick on a throw from your weak hand, snatching the ball as it peaks (above left and right) and put it back into the cascade.

HOT TIP

The arc of the snatched ball should be higher than the normal cascade, the catch - if taken at the peak of the trajectory - will give you more time to bring the ball down, turn your hand round and execute a normal throw.

Try it with the other hand – be ambidextrous! Then you can attempt to snatch every throw with both hands; you will need to transfer the ball with a palm-down action – a flick – which will put a spin on the ball. Remember to pitch each throw higher than the normal cascade pattern.

WARNING

This trick will seriously impress everybody!

The Chop

FOR CHOPS we go straight into using two balls, one in each hand. Why? Because you deserve it!

1 With your strong hand raised to its highest point in the plane of the "sheet of glass", throw the other ball in a normal arc, **but**, as it ascends, bring your arm down towards the central axis of your body (below left), so the moving ball travels under the arm (below). This movement can be done quite slowly at first.

2 When your strong hand reaches the lower level of the "sheet of glass" it releases its ball with a little hop towards the other hand (right).

3   The strong hand then quickly returns to catch the descending first ball, which is still in its normal arc (above right).

4   Now while juggling with three balls, pitch a throw slightly higher with your weak hand, catch the ball at the top of the arc with your strong hand, bring it down – arm straight – and into the centre of the pattern, with the next throw travelling underneath as you have just learned.

HOT TIP

The next throw with your weak hand should be higher than normal to give some time for the little hop after the chop, and to catch the higher ball.

With practice the downward movement of the straight arm will become faster, like a karate chop through the air. Be ambidextrous, and continuous – now you're getting seriously hot!

The Shower

CAST YOUR mind back to learning *the cascade* with two balls. We said you must only throw the ball *up*, not pass it from one hand to the other by the short route. This time, that's exactly what you have to do. If you were doing this before, it wasn't wrong, you just weren't ready for it...Now you are!

1   Take two balls, one in each hand and do that school yard thing. Toss a ball into the air as an *over the top* throw with your strong hand, and pass the other ball by the short route to the strong hand. Actually it's more of a slap of the ball from one hand to the other.

2 Now for three balls. Take two in your strong hand and just go for it (page 42). As soon as you have thrown the first ball, send the second up following the same path as the first, and slap the third into your empty strong hand (left).

HOT TIP

As always <u>count out loud</u>, and remember the first two balls go right behind each other. There are two balls in the air at any one time! Yeah, it's harder than the normal cascade, but it's the way most people try to learn without the aid of this book - so it's got to be done. Don't forget to try it the other way round too!

Two Classic Three-Ball Tricks

The Statue Of Liberty

THIS IS a variation of the shower. Raise your weaker hand, arm straight, rather like the pose of the famous Statue of Liberty in New York harbour. Now throw a ball from your strong hand up to that hand, catching it palm up (below). The hand should be tilted inwards to tip the ball down again, so the other hand can catch it, waist high. Build up with a ball in each hand (below), leading to a shower with three balls.

HOT TIP

The raised hand should hardly move; concentrate on those throws!

Overhead

Find a space with a bit of headroom, lean back your head and with a ball in your strong hand, palm up, hand raised to shoulder height, push the ball up and over to the other hand. The catching hand must be in the same position as the throwing hand. Now build up the trick with two balls, and finally three (above).

HOT TIP

If the balls constantly go forwards, tip your head back more to compensate.

Having a Three-Ball Ball

A Fancy Start

YOU CAN juggle three balls with ease and confidently put in a few tricks, so what about an impressive way to start a pattern?

1   Take two balls in your strong hand – this time they should rest alongside each other, not one in front of the other (below).

2   Throw them in the air at the same time so they split up and rise, both to the same height (right).

3   As both balls peak in their arc, the third ball in the other hand is thrown up between them (right), as in the *one-up two-up* pattern.

4   The two balls are caught with a delay (far right), like in One up Two up, and then the third ball is included in a three-ball cascade.

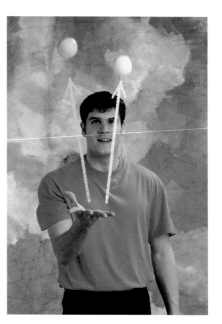

HOT TIP

When throwing the two balls together, roll them off the hand either side of the middle finger, which splits them apart so that the next throw can come up the middle.

To make this trick more dramatic, you can hide the first throw by bringing your other arm horizontally across your body (right), hiding the throwing hand.

The Neck Catch

SO YOU have a start, now you need a flashy finish. The neck catch is the most impressive.

1 Throw a high throw (not too high at first) and bend your body forward from the waist.
2 With the other balls one in each hand, push your arms out to the sides (below). This should form a "v" shape with your head up and facing forward.
3 The ball will be trapped as it falls into a nice dip made by your shoulder blades and head – the shoulders will funnel the ball into exactly the right position (right).

HOT TIP

The ball should be thrown vertically and **not** behind you. Your head tips forward to meet the ball as it drops.

You can go back into the three-ball cascade from here by dipping your head down and quickly flicking it back up, which in turn flicks the ball up and back into the pattern.

Using the Body

AS WITH all the tricks you have learned so far, try this with just one ball first. Popping a ball off some part of your body is fun and makes for an impressive trick. The easiest option is to bounce a ball off your knee. Throw a normal arc, bring your knee up and fire the ball back to the original hand (right). With practice this can be done with any part of the body (below): the elbow, wrist, foot, forehead, whatever. My favourite – after a high throw gather up the bottom of your T-shirt with both hands, then catch and "trampoline" the ball back into the pattern.

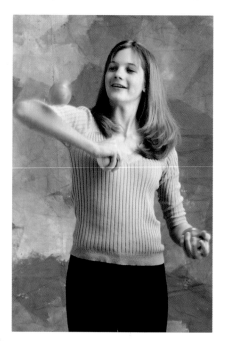

Stage 4

THERE'S MORE TO LIFE THAN THREE BALLS

Crazy for Numbers

I THINK JUGGLING large numbers of objects is over-rated, but that's because I can't do it! The world record for juggling balls is 11. Me, I stick at five.

Four Balls

When juggling two balls in one hand you learned to throw anti-clockwise with the left hand and clockwise with the right (see pages 34–35). To juggle that fourth ball, just throw two balls in both hands (top left, page 53)! Don't the balls cross over? No, both sides stay in the plane of their own sheet of glass.

HOT TIP

Make sure first that you are solid juggling two balls with your weak hand. If the balls tend to cross, juggle with your hands either side of an open door; wayward balls hit the door and go back into the pattern!

The hands can either throw in-sync or out-of-sync, making columns or circular patterns. Four ways to juggle four balls!

Five Balls

1 Have five balls of the same size and weight.

2 Place three in your stronger hand, and two in the other.

3 The balls cross as a normal cascade, only slightly higher to give extra time to deal with them (top right). All the normal rules apply: count out loud, stay in the jugglespace, etc. Try just throwing the balls without catching them and they should land on the floor in two neat clusters of three and two.

HOT TIP

Learn standing over a bed: there will be a lot more drops than normal, so save your back! Don't panic - the pattern is always slower than you think. Your muscles will build up to maintain the rhythm and consistent throws needed to master this routine.

Juggling with Clubs

YOU WILL have seen people juggling clubs – a lot of people into performance, competition and social juggling use them. That's because juggling with clubs looks large and impressive. Unfortunately you have to learn to juggle all over again. Don't believe me? Pick up a set of clubs and give it a whirl. Ouch!

We now have to learn to spin an object. A club is a clever thing. It's big opposite the handle so that as it spins about its centre of gravity (about two-thirds of the way down) the clubhead misses the catching hand, avoiding injury, presenting the handle to be caught easily.

First hold the club in your strong hand (below left), near the top of

the handle, not right at the knob end. Give it a few spins to the same hand and get the feel of how it performs (bottom right, page 54). Bulbous clubs tend to spin slower.

Now take a look at your hand: palm up, thumb at right angles to the index finger. The club must be caught across the palm so the fingers can close on the handle. I know that sounds so obvious, but it's not the same as juggling with balls. When you flip it to the other hand, the club should point out to the side of the body at the angle made by the position of the hand, palm up, with the elbows at the side in a relaxed juggling stance. To achieve this, when throwing the club sweep it down and throw across your lower body (below left) – this presents it neatly into the waiting hand (below right).

Juggling with Clubs

FOR THE next step you have a choice. Some say "take two clubs" and follow the rules as in two balls. I recommend that you take one club and one ball and concentrate on making accurate throws with the club (below).

Once you are proficient you can either add the third club or second ball (below). If you chose the ball method, then, after you have practised for some time (right inset), replace each ball with a club (right).

HOT TIP

If you try to throw the club in the same arc as a ball you may end up having to twist your hand through 90 degrees to catch it. OK for the odd catch but not every one!

Juggling with Rings

JUGGLING RINGS look very good visually – some people find them better for high-numbers juggling, and they have special tricks of their own.

Rings, like clubs, require a different way of catching and throwing. Grip the ring in your hand with your thumb on top (below). Throw it to your strong hand, dipping the hand down and releasing the ring with your palm up. Catch it with your palm up and your thumb and index finger facing back towards you (below). Then follow the same sequence as for learning club juggling (right).

HOT TIP

To avoid collisions the ring must be thrown without any twists, turns or wobbles in their flight. A good throw with a bit of spin on it is what is required.

How to Juggle with Anything

IF YOU have learned the three styles of juggling – balls, clubs and rings – you can juggle absolutely anything. You just have to work out which of the three styles is appropriate to the object you have chosen. It helps to get used to juggling things that are a mixture of different weights – if you followed my advice by learning clubs and balls mixed, you will already be halfway there.

Here are some hints, although obviously the list is endless. The shape of the object usually gives it away.

Fruit and vegetables: a cucumber or a banana is a club; just about anything else is a ball. **Kitchen implements:** those with handles are clubs; plates are rings. Special juggling knives are carefully balanced so it's *not* a

good idea to use the ordinary kitchen variety for juggling unless you too are very sharp – mistakes can hurt (ouch!).

Tennis rackets, guitars, umbrellas: ...and other long things are all clubs. We talked about the centre of gravity when we learned about clubs (see pages 54–55): objects with a centre of gravity about two-thirds of the way along from the catching end juggle best.

Scarves: juggling silk scarves can be very graceful. You treat them like balls (but you throw them higher because they spend longer in the air); you have to snatch them instead of catching them normally.

Frisbees, tyres, wheels: rings, of course.

This book: it's a ring, isn't it? It might help if you taped the cover together so it doesn't flap about. Then off you go!

Put the Book Down!

YOU HAVE finished this book, but there is much much more that you can learn about juggling, and lots of places to find out. The best source is other jugglers. Many cities have juggling workshops that meet weekly where people swap tricks and ideas. Universities and colleges are often good places to start looking. If there isn't a workshop or club

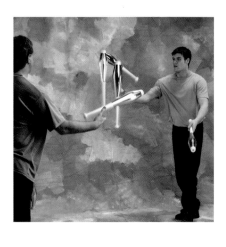

in your town, get a few friends together and start one!

Every year there are juggling conventions throughout Europe and the USA, including big national and international ones where hundreds or even thousands of jugglers of all abilities meet to have fun and maybe throw a few things in the air too. There are also many local city conventions. A good place to find out about these is The Juggling Information Service which is on the Internet at <www.juggling.org>, where you will also find interesting links and places to meet other jugglers online. It's an American site but pretty global in its outlook.

One of the most sociable things jugglers do is club passing: two or more people making a juggling pattern together. It's too big a subject to start with in this book, but it is pretty easy to pick up with a few friends. On the net, a lot of jugglers communicate about patterns in a special notation called siteswap. Basically it describes each throw by a number that corresponds to how many balls you'd be juggling if every throw were like that: the three-ball cascade is 333, not throwing a ball is 0. You'll find a more complete explanation online.

A good source of UK information is Butterfingers, who also happen to be the largest wholesalers of juggling and circus equipment in the country. They are at:
Unit 10, Burnett Business Park,
Gypsy Lane,
Burnett,
Keynsham,
Bristol BS31 2ED
tel 0117-986-6680
fax 0117-986-6690
mailbox@butterfingers.co.uk

This book is only intended as a beginning. There's a whole world of juggling out there. Put the book down and go and find some!

Further Reading

IF YOUR appetite for juggling books has been whetted by our little volume, you can find more tricks than you would ever want to learn in Charlie Dancey's *Encyclopedia of Ball Juggling* and his *Compendium of Club Juggling*, both of which are published by Butterfingers.

At the moment there is not a British juggling or circus magazine on the market (but keep your ears open!). The European perspective is covered pretty efficiently by *Kaskade*. It does not have a great deal about Britain in it, but it's good for tricks and European events.

It is published in a bilingual English/German edition from:
Schonbergstr.92,
D-65199 Wiesbaden,
Germany
tel (+49) 611-946-5142
fax (+49) 611-946-5143
kaskade@compuserve.com